Mayumi Kobayashi
Translation

David Hair
Interview Translation

Eve Grandt and Melissa DeJesus
Retouch and Lettering

Vanessa Satone
Designer

Stephen Pakula
Production Manager

Mike Lackey
Director of Print Production

Stephanie Shalofsky
Vice President, Production

John O'Donnell
Publisher

World Peace Through Shared Popular Culture™

centralparkmedia.com

cpmpress.com

World of Narue Book 1. Published by CPM Manga, a division of Central Park Media Corporation. Office of Publication – 250 West 57th Street, Suite 317, New York, NY 10107. Original Japanese version "The World of Narue Book 1" © TOMOHIRO MARUKAWA 2000. Originally published in Japan in 2000 by KADOKAWA SHOTEN PUBLISHING Co.,Ltd.. English translation rights arranged with KADOKAWA SHOTEN PUBLISHING Co.,Ltd., Tokyo through TOHAN CORPORATION, TOKYO. English version © 2004 Central Park Media Corporation. CPM Manga and logo are registered trademarks of Central Park Media Corporation. Original Manga and logo are trademarks of Central Park Media Corporation. All rights reserved. Price per copy $9.99, price in Canada may vary. ISBN: 1-58664-961-2. Catalog number: CMX 66001G. UPC: 7-19987-00660-7-00111. Printed in Canada.

THE WORLD OF NARUE

Book One

Story and Art by

Tomohiro Marukawa

CPM® MANGA

New York, New York

Contents

Character Profiles

Narue Nanase

Narue is not your average 14-year-old girl. Although born and raised on Earth, Narue is actually half-alien! Living on Earth hasn't made it easier for Narue to gain friends, though. She has avoided earthlings for a long time, so her friends have been few and far between. When Narue finally opens up to an earthling boy named Kazuto, their adventures together begin.

Kazuto Izuka

Gentle by nature, and a good friend and confidant. Although leery of Narue at first, he soon discovers there is more to her than he realizes. Kazuto is also a fan of anime.

Kazuto Izuka

Narue Nanase

Maruo

Kazuto's best friend and classmate, Maruo is the son of a local fish merchant. Maruo is also the next-door neighbor and childhood friend of Hajime.

Hajime Yagi

Childhood friend of Maruo, Hajime is known for her fascination with science fiction and the paranormal. Despite her hobbies, she does not believe Narue is actually an alien.

Kanaka Nanase

Kanaka is actually Narue's older sister, despite the fact that she looks like she is 12 years old. She is strong-willed and finds it difficult to act sisterly towards Narue. Kanaka is 100% alien, sharing the same father as Narue.

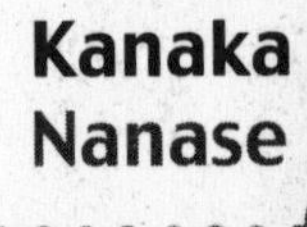

Kanaka Nanase

Hajime Yagi

A REALLY NICE GUY WOULD--
--PUT DOWN HIS UMBRELLA, GET WET AND SAVE YOU.
KWOO

THEN SOME GIRL WOULD WALK BY AND SAY--
FSSSS
YOU'RE SO SWEET, KAZUTO!
--AND GET ALL MUSHY.
THIS ISN'T A SHOJO MANGA.
CHOP
SELF-KARATE CHOP!

MOVE!!
STARTLE
IT'S A TRAP!

CHAPTER I : THE WORLD OF NARUE

WHAT DO YOU MEAN "TRAP"?
SWING
GSSH
VSH

ARR...
ARR...
THIS IS A DANGEROUS ALTERED SPACE ORGANISM.
DRIBBLE
DRIBBLE

YOU LUCKED OUT!
SHE WAS WEARING MY SCHOOL'S UNIFORM.
FSSSSS
SPLASH
ON A RAINY EVENING, IN FRONT OF A RUNDOWN APARTMENT BUILDING --
--I FELL IN LOVE WITH A MYSTERIOUS GIRL.

HEH
HEH
HEH
KAZUTO, DID I EVER TELL YA YOU'RE A POET?
SLAM
YOU'RE A *POET*!
SLAM

I DON'T KNOW IF SHE SAVED ME FROM GETTING RABIES OR THE EBOLA VIRUS, BUT SHE SAVED ME!
F...FELL IN LOVE ...
HEH HEH HEH.
SHUT UP AND CHECK THE ATTENDANCE SHEETS.

SHE FORGOT THIS BAT, AND IT'S THE ONLY CLUE I HAVE.
Narue
YEAH, YEAH.

FOUND IT.
SHE'S IN THE CLASS NEXT TO OURS. SECOND YEAR, CLASS TWO.
GOOD JOB, MARUO!

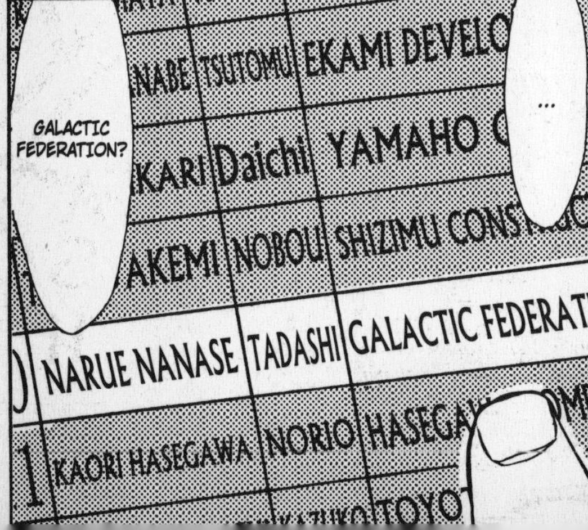
...
GALACTIC FEDERATION?
NABE TSUTOMU EKAMI DEVELO
KARI Daichi YAMAHO
AKEMI NOBOU SHIZIMU CONSTRUCT
NARUE NANASE TADASHI GALACTIC FEDERATI
KAORI HASEGAWA NORIO HASEGA
KAZUKO TOYOT

SHE'S AN INVADER FROM SPACE?
BOOM
MAYBE SHE'S A SPACE PILOT!
WOOOSH
OVER THERE! OVER THERE!
TAK
THAT'S HER!
TAK
DAMN, SHE'S A HUMANOID.
HUH?
JUST GIMME THE BAT.
I CAN'T HEAR YOU!
YES, SIR!
ARE YOU A PANSY?
NO, SIR!
LISTEN, YOUR NEW NAME IS "LOVE HUNTER"!
FWOOM
Y... YES, SIR...
CAN YOU ASK HER OUT YOURSELF?
YES, SIR!
OKAY! HERE'S THE BAT!
THANK YOU, SIR!!

LOVE HUNTER, GO GET'EM!!
GAH HA HA
ONE OF THESE DAYS I'M GONNA KILL HIM.

TAK
WAIT! MS. NANASE!
TAK

YES, THAT'S ME.
PAT
AAAH!!

WHAT?
? ?
HUH? WASN'T SHE IN FRONT?

THANK YOU FOR SAVING ME YESTER-DAY.
Blush
UM, WOULD YOU LIKE TO GO OUT FOR COFFEE SOMETIME?
ARE YOU TELLING ME TO TAKE YOU OUT FOR COFFEE BECAUSE YOU'RE RETURNING MY BAT?
マニュアルどおり
Typical Pick Up Line
完全に例外
Completely Oblivious
HEY.
FWOOOOOOOOO
Bzz
Bzz
THERE'S NO NEED TO CRY.

WHAT'S YOUR NAME?
KAZUTO!
KAZUTO IZUKA!
YOU'D BE BORED OUT OF YOUR MIND WITH ME.
WHAT?
THAT'S NOT TRUE!
EVEN IF I'M CHEAP AND RECLU-SIVE?
YEAH.
EVEN IF I LOVE READING THE WEEKLY TABLOIDS?
Y... YEAH.
TABLOID...
EVEN IF MY FATHER'S AN ALIEN?
YEAH.
HUH?
GRAB

GAHH!
LET'S GO TO MY HOUSE. IT'LL BE CHEAPER THAN GOING TO A CAFE.
CALL ME NARUE, KAZUTO.
ズルズル DRAG DRAG
ズル DRAG
NARUE ... CAN'T ... BREATHE ...
YES, KAZUTO?
ぐいっ
すたすた TOK TOK
HERE WE ARE. THIS IS MY HOUSE.
HEY, IT'S THE RUN-DOWN APARTMENT FROM THE OTHER DAY!
TINK TINK
I'M SO EMBARRASSED, MY HOUSE IS SUCH A MESS.
ぶんぶん SWING SWING
?

AAH!
sigh
ほへ～
THIS DOORPLATE HAS SO MUCH CHARACTER.
Galactic Communication Base
Tadashi & Narue Nanase
チャラ
Galactic Communication Base
Tadashi & Narue Nanase
WHAT'S WRONG?
SIGH...
TWP.
チャポン
DAA!
DAD!
SL-
DIDN'T I TELL YOU TO *RETURN* THE EMPTY MILK BOTTLE!?
-AM

A BURGLER!
HUH?
NARUE. OHHHH...
HUH?
HE'S AN ABALONIAN FROM THE CYGNUS CONSTELLATION N SYSTEM EE (UNPRONOUNCEABLE).
THUD
HE'S A SPACE NINJA.
DAUGHTER OF NANASE!
I'M IMPRESSED YOU'VE FIGURED OUT MY TRAP!
Cygnus Constellation (in Short) Abalonian

WHAT SHOULD WE DO? IF WE PROVOKE HIM...
BUT...
Clinch
IF I DON'T SAVE NARUE, I'D BE A COWARD!
DASH
RAHHHHH

TRIP
SL..
..AM
WHO'S THE KID?
THUMP
THUMP
HE GOT ME WOR-RIED FOR A SEC.
AAAAAA AAA...
TAKE YOUR SHOES OFF WHEN YOU GO INSIDE.
OW! WHY'D YOU DO *THAT* FOR?
wake

I'M JOKING.
THANKS.
!!
HEH HEH HEH!
FS
SOB
I'LL KILL THE OLD MAN FIRST.
EH HEH HEH HEH
YOU'RE UNDER ARREST!

JUST KIDDING.
DONK
SSSSSSS
THUD

PHEW. THANKS.
...
DAD,
YOU NEED TO BE MORE CAREFUL.
MR. COWARD.
TWITCH TWITCH
WE SHOULD CALL THE POLICE, NO, AN AMBU-LANCE.
THE NINJA'S FINE.
BUT I REALLY THINK HE'S JUST A GUY.

YOU SAID YOU DON'T MIND IF I'M AN ALIEN, RIGHT?
YEAH, AND YOU LIKE WEEKLY TABLOIDS, RIGHT? SHOULD I START READING THEM TOO?
...
LET ME SHOW YOU SOME-THING.
GRAB
AH.

VVVM
!
VVVM

WELCOME TO ***OUR*** WORLD.

KAZUTO.

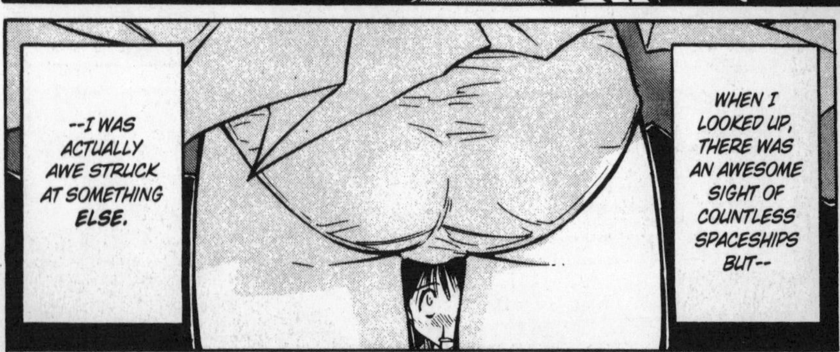

End of Chapter

REMEMBER THAT GIRL NAMED NARUE NANASE THAT I ASKED MARUO TO HELP ME FIND?
WHEN I ASKED HER OUT SHE SAID OKAY!
NARUE'S REALLY STRONG.
SHE CAN BEAT UP A BURGLAR USING TELEPORTATION!
SHE SHOWED ME A FLEET OF AMAZING SPACESHIPS.
PLEASE BE MY DAUGHTER'S FRIEND.
HERE TAKE MY CARD.
DAD!
お父さ～ん
I FOUND OUT HER FATHER IS A MEMBER OF THE EARTH INVESTIGATION TEAM OF THE GALACTIC FEDERATION!

SOMETIMES I CAN'T TELL WHAT SHE'S THINKING BUT--
--IT'S OKAY. SHE'S AN ALIEN!
Chapter 2: WHAT'S WRONG WITH FALLING IN LOVE?

CLANK
CRASH
THUD
AN ALIEN?
AND WE ARE --
--GOING ON A DATE TOMORROW.

...AND HER BOYFRIEND SKI BOARDS BUT HE WEARS HIS CELL AROUND HIS NECK BECAUSE HE'S AFRAID HE'LL LOSE IT.
HAH HAH.
THAT'S SO LAME.

I'D NEVER BE CAUGHT DEAD WITH A GUY LIKE THAT.
YEAH.
FFT
FFT

NARUE, DO YOU HAVE A BOY-FRIEND?
HUH?
SHE'S A FRIENDLESS ALIEN. SHE DOESN'T HAVE A BOYFRIEND!

BUT I SAW HER WITH A GUY. HE HAD EIGHT LEGS!
HAH
HAH
きゃははは

NARUE, ARE YOU HERE?
YOU HAVE A VISITOR!

KAZUTO!
WHAT?
YEAH

SORRY.
YOU MUST HAVE SEEN SOMEONE ELSE WITH THE EIGHT-LEGGED GUY.

STOP TRYING TO ACT SO TOUGH.
THUMP
THUMP
I BETTER FIND A BOY-FRIEND TOO!
I KNEW IT WAS YOU.

WHAT'S UP?
IT'S ABOUT TOMORROW.

UM, WE'RE MEETING IN FRONT OF THE STATION AT NOON, RIGHT?
I'M LOOKING FORWARD TO IT.

翌日 よくじつ THE NEXT DAY
WHERE DO YOU WANT TO GO?
LET'S GET A BITE TO EAT.
NacdoNalds
220

THE 100 YEN BURGER SALE --
--IS OVER.
YES, WE'RE REALLY SORRY.

CAN YOU GIVE ME A DISCOUNT?
I'M SORRY. I CAN'T.

I FORGOT NARUE WAS A CHEAPSKATE.
SLURP
180 YEN ...

I'LL PAY FOR IT.
NO! THE FINANCES OF A RELATIONSHIP SHOULD BE EQUALLY SPLIT!

NEXT STOP IS THE DATING HOT STOP!
180 YEN ...
WE HAVE TO HAVE FUN THERE!

IT'S FAST!
IT'S GOING TOO FAST!!
IRRR!
DSH
WHY?
BEEEP
BAD
DANCE
DANCE
NARUE, I THINK THAT'S ENOUGH.
I WANT A REMATCH!
KACHI

MACKERELLY
Chuco Place
SHE FELL ASLEEP.
LOOK! IT'S MACKEREL! MACKEREL EVERY-WHERE!
SPLISH SPLISH
MACK-ERELLY IS COMING ...
ZZZ
MACK-ERELLY?
TADAA

BUT SHE WAS GOING NUTS AT THE ARCADE.

!!
THUMP
NNN...
DON'T KICK! I SAID DON'T KICK!
KICK KICK

IT'S A LARGE CATCH!
SPLISHHH
IT'S MADE ITS WAY OVER THE DEFENSE LINE!

I'M SORRY!

I'LL TAKE YOU SOMEPLACE REALLY NICE TO MAKE IT UP TO YOU.

TUG

SHE'S CHANGING THE SUBJECT.

VREEN

WHERE ARE WE?
AT THE BASE OF THE KISO MOUNTAIN RANGE IN NAGANO PREFECTURE. I THINK WE'RE ABOUT SIX HUNDRED METERS ALTITUDE.

LIE DOWN.
HUH?

LOOK AT THE STARS. DO YOU LIKE LOOKING FOR CONSTEL-LATIONS?
RUSTLE

ARE YOU THINKING SOMETHING NAUGHTY?
OF COURSE NOT.

I WAS BORN ON EARTH SO I LIKE THE STARS, BUT I DON'T LIKE THEM AT NIGHT BECAUSE THEY'RE SO FAR AWAY.
THE MOON LOOKS LIKE A GIANT STONE FROM HERE.
NO MATTER HOW BEAUTIFUL THE NIGHT SKY IS, I CLOSE MY EYES AND SIT STILL.
WE DIDN'T HAVE TO COME HERE IF YOU WEREN'T GOING TO LOOK AT ANYTHING.
WHEN I SIT UNDER THE NIGHT SKY WHEN THERE'S NO MOON OR STARS, I FEEL LIKE IT'S ONLY THE EARTH AND ME.
FWOOOOOO

DO YOU THINK THAT'S STRANGE?

ARE YOU COLD?
NO, I'M OKAY.

I'LL TRY IT TOO.

RUSTLE
...

I SEE THINGS GLITTERING EVEN WITH MY EYES CLOSED.
THEY LOOK LIKE STARS.

AH!
SQUEEZE

NARUE'S HAND--

--IS SO WARM.

FWOOOO

INSPECTIO
BUREAU

YOU HAVE GAINED KAZUTO IZUKA'S HEART.
IS THAT SUPPOSED TO BE SARCASM?

EXCEPT FOR MINIMAL PERSONAL EXPENDITURES, I HAVE NOT GIVEN NOR GAINED ANYTHING.

IT'S GOING TO BE TOUGH, NARUE. ONE DAY YOU MUST DECIDE BETWEEN THIS PLANET AND US.

FOR-GIVE ME.

THERE WILL BE NO MORE INSPEC-TIONS.
...
TOK

End of Chapter

NARUE NANASE IS A REAL ALIEN BUT--
SEE YOU LATER, ALIEN!
--NO ONE EVER SEEMED TO CARE.
BYE-BYE, KAZUTO!
EXCEPT FOR THIS GIRL.
NARUE'S NOT AN ALIEN!!
THAT GOES AGAINST EVERYTHING--
--I KNOW COMPLETELY!

CHAPTER 3: NARUE'S TRUE IDENTITY

SHE'S HAJIME YAGI, THE SCI-FI GURU, A.K.A. "THE WALKING X-FILES."

SHE'S JUST AS MUCH AS A WEIRDO AS NARUE.

BEEP
HAJIME? IT'S MOM.
NARUE PISSES ME OFF.
HOW IS SHE SUPPOSED TO BE AN ALIEN?
KCH KCH KCH
I'M ON A BUSINESS TRIP RIGHT NOW AND I'M CALLING FROM INSIDE--
--A BULLET TRAIN. GET WHATEVER FOR DINNER--
--AND I'LL PAY YOU BACK. I'LL BE BACK IN TWO DAYS. BYE.
SLAM

ON NIGHTS LIKE THIS--
--IT'S BEST TO LOOK AT THE STARS.
SLIDE
HEY, HAJIME.
EEEK
STRUMM

WHY ARE YOU HERE?
I WAS LED BY THE STARS.
HAH
VREEEEEM

WHY DOES EVERYONE TRY TO MAKE A FOOL OUT OF ME?
SLAM
HUH?

WHO'S EVERY-ONE?
VREEEEM

...

KAZUTO, CAN YOU HIDE ME IN THIS CLASSROOM DURING LUNCH?

SURE, SIT DOWN.

WHAT'S WRONG?

THERE'S SOMEONE ANNOY-ING...

NWARUE NWANWASE!

STOMP

STOMP

NARUE'S ONLY TRYING TO GET *ATTENTION*--
--BY SAYING SHE'S AN *ALIEN*.

YOU'RE COMPLETELY FOOLED BY NARUE'S SELF-SCRIPTED, SELF-ACTING PLAY.
EH?

DO YOU HAVE PROOF TO PROVE ME *WRONG*?
I DO.
BUT IT'S SUPPOSED TO BE A SECRET.

PLANET NIPPON GUIDEBOOK?
PLANET NIPPON
GUIDEBOOK
1
PART 1
OUR HISTORY
IT'S A BOOK ABOUT MY DAD'S PLANET.

PLANET?
HOW DID ...
PLANET JAPAN
GUIDEBOOK
PART 1
COMMADORE PERRY'S ARRIVAL
MEIJI RESTORATION
THE SUN'S RAYS ARE HOT
WWII DEFEAT

TO *HELL* WITH THIS!

SLAM

I THINK IT'S BETTER IF YOU EXPLAIN IT TO HER.

I COULD CARE LESS WHAT PEOPLE THINK AS LONG AS *YOU* KNOW.

...
AS FAR AS I CAN TELL --
--EXCEPT FOR HER WEIRD HAIRSTYLE --
-- SHE'S AN ORDINARY HUMAN.
ARE YOU LUSTING OVER ME?
GET YOUR MIND OUT OF THE GUTTER!

BAM
BAM
IF YOU'RE AN ALIEN--
--DODGE THIS!
...
THROW
TAKE THIS! AND THIS!
WHOA!
THROW THROW THROW
DODGE
SHOCK
WHAT!?
Dodge
Dodge

HA-HA!
YOU CAN'T GET ME...
Thrash
I KNEW YOU WERE HUMAN!
BASEBALL
YOU'RE SUCH AN IDIOT!
あはははは
Hah hah hah hah hah hah hah

STEP

DONK

SLAM

SHE HIT THE BACK OF HER HEAD!

SHE'S BLEEDING!

NARUE.

I THINK YOU SHOULD STAY AWAY FROM HAJIME.

YEAH.

I PLAN TO.

AH!
BLEE!
BLEE!
HOW TIRING.
DIDN'T YOU JUST SAY...
TOK
I WONDER WHY SHE WANTS TO KNOW MY IDENTITY.
I WONDER WHAT IT REALLY IS--
--THAT MAKES HER SO MAD?

I COULD CARE LESS WHAT PEOPLE THINK--
--AS LONG AS YOU KNOW.
I'M FINE--
--BY MYSELF.

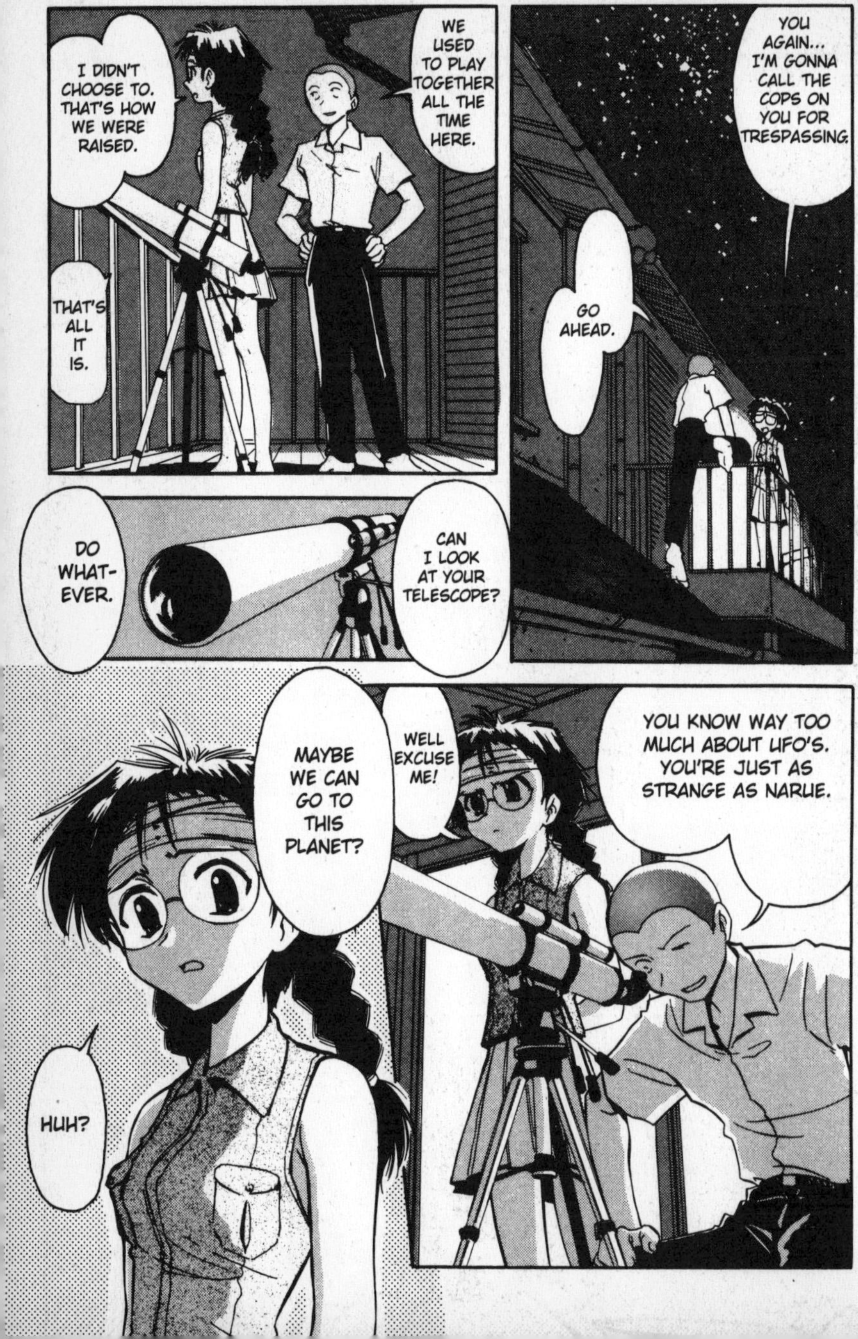

YOU AGAIN... I'M GONNA CALL THE COPS ON YOU FOR TRESPASSING.
GO AHEAD.

WE USED TO PLAY TOGETHER ALL THE TIME HERE.
I DIDN'T CHOOSE TO. THAT'S HOW WE WERE RAISED.
THAT'S ALL IT IS.

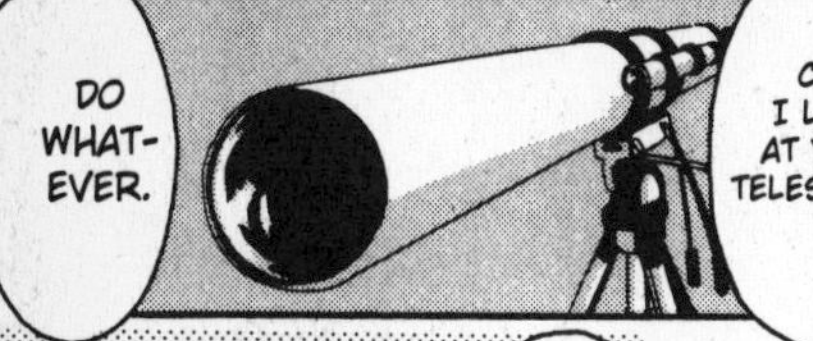
CAN I LOOK AT YOUR TELESCOPE?
DO WHAT-EVER.

YOU KNOW WAY TOO MUCH ABOUT UFO'S. YOU'RE JUST AS STRANGE AS NARUE.
WELL EXCUSE ME!
MAYBE WE CAN GO TO THIS PLANET?
HUH?

End of Chapter

KAZUTO IZUKA IS HEAD OVER HEELS FOR NARUE NANASE.
NARUE'S AN ALIEN, SO HER LIFE IS VERY COMPLICATED.
PERHAPS IT MIGHT BE BLAMED ON HER UPBRINGING, BUT SHE HASN'T HAD A FRIEND THE FIRST FOURTEEN YEARS OF LIFE.
ONE DAY, KAZUTO INVITED NARUE OVER TO HIS HOUSE.
NARUE NANASE, FOUR-TEEN YEARS OLD.
SHE COULDN'T HAVE BEEN HAPPIER.

CHAPTER 4: DANCER IN THE DARK
THANK YOU! I'M COMING IN!
SLAM

KAZUTO'S HOUSE.
KLANK
HOME.
HOME.

THIS IS MY ROOM.

YOU HAVE A COMPUTER! YOU'RE SO HIGH-CLASS!
NO. I SAVED UP AND I WAS FINALLY ABLE TO BUY IT.

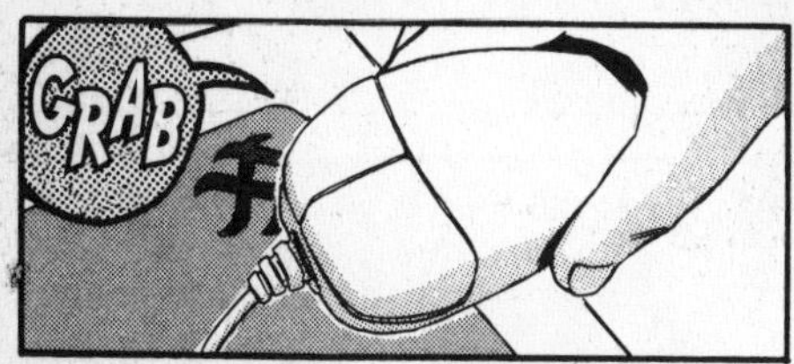
GRAB

HELLO? HELLO?
RESPOND, COMPUTER.

HUH?
TWEET
TWEET

SWIP
HAA!
THERE'S NO NEED TO SCREAM.
SIGH
SWISH
SWISH

AH!
VREEM
I'M SORRY! COME BACK!

I HATE MACHINES.
VREEE
THEN I'LL TEACH YOU.
PHEW

GRAB THAT.
CLICK
CLICK
NOT THAT.
THAT ONE.
HUH?
CLICK
CLICK
RATTLE

YOU DID IT!
FLASH

YOU REALLY ARE BAD WITH COMPUTERS.
YEAH.

DO YOU LIKE WHALES?
YEAH,
THEY'RE COOL.

I'M SO GLAD I HAD A PICTURE.
CRY
FLASH
WHAT'S THIS?

AAAAH!!

I'M LEAVING.
WAIT!
IT'S MY FRIEND'S CD!

WAIT HERE. I'LL GO MAKE SOME TEA.
FRIEND?

IT'S NORMAL, I GUESS.
HE'S A BOY.
PLOP

YUKI—
...

FWUMP

SUDDENLY THE ROOM FEELS DIRTY.

STARTLE
CLK

VREEE
HUH?

SIGH ...
WHAT A SREW-UP ...
TAK
KAZUTO! KAZUTO!
TAK TAK
!!
EEK

WHAT DID YOU SEE *THIS* TIME?
SOME-THING'S WRONG WITH YOUR COMPUTER.
TREMBLE

IT'S NOT BROKEN.
fweee
THIS COMES ON AFTER YOU LEAVE THE COMPUTER ALONE FOR WHILE.

IT'S A PROGRAM THAT KEEPS THE IMAGES FROM GET-TING BURNT ONTO THE MONITOR.
OH...
fwee

IT CAME ON ALL ON IT'S OWN.
IT SCARED ME.
IT'S CALLED A SCREEN-SAVER.

WHO'S THE DANCING GIRL?
YOU DON'T KNOW?

SHE'S FROM AN ANIME. BLITZ GIRL AUSF-CHAN.
BLITZ GIRL
IV Ausf H
chan
THE BATTLE SCENES ARE AWESOME.

YOU LIKE IT?
YEAH.
YOU'RE SUCH AN OTAKU.

ポリポリ
MUNCH MUNCH

SHP
YEAH. A PRESENT.
I HAVE TO GIVE SOME-THING BACK.

I HAVE AN IDEA!
DAD, CAN I USE THE SUPER INTERSPACE TELE-COMMUNI-CATIONS?
I'D RATHER YOU NOT BECAUSE THEY CHARGE AN ARM AND A LEG.

DON'T WORRY. IT'S A LOCAL CALL--
--AND I'M ONLY SENDING AN IMAGE.
EARTH
JAPANESE
ST&T
ANSWERABLE
CLICK
VWOO

UHH? HOW DO I USE THIS AGAIN?
HELP ME, DAD!

I'M NOT GOING TO HELP IF IT'S FOR PERSONAL USE.
AW ...
COME ON! DON'T BE SO MEAN!

WHAT'S WRONG?
IS IT A BURGLAR?
Dad 父
mom 母
older sis 姉
NO.
IT'S NOTHING.
WHAT IS IT?!
WHAT IS IT?!
NARUE!
TRA
LA
LA
IT'S LATE!
YOU CAN'T BE HERE!
TWIRL
TWIRL
!
FSSS

IT'S A--
--HOLO-GRAM?!

WOW. IT LOOKS SO **REAL**.
PLOP
ポスッ

フィーーーーン
fweeee
...

IS SHE --
ハッ
AH
--TRYING TO IMITATE AUSF-CHAN?

SHE'S SO STRANGE.
WHATEVER. THERE'S NO HARM IN IT, I GUESS.

FLIP
FLIP
BLLL
IT'S--
--HAZARDOUS TO MY HEALTH!
DRIP
DRIP

I'M SO HAPPY!
I'LL TAKE GOOD CARE OF IT!
...
DAMN IT!
GRAB
I'M NOT HAPPY AT ALL!
I'M SO HAPPY!
I'LL TAKE GOOD CARE OF IT!
HUH? BUT IT'S ONLY A PICTURE PRINT OUT.
THAT'S NOT IT.

WHAT'S IMPORTANT IS THAT SOMEONE GAVE IT TO ME.
THAT'S WHY IT MEANS SO MUCH TO ME.

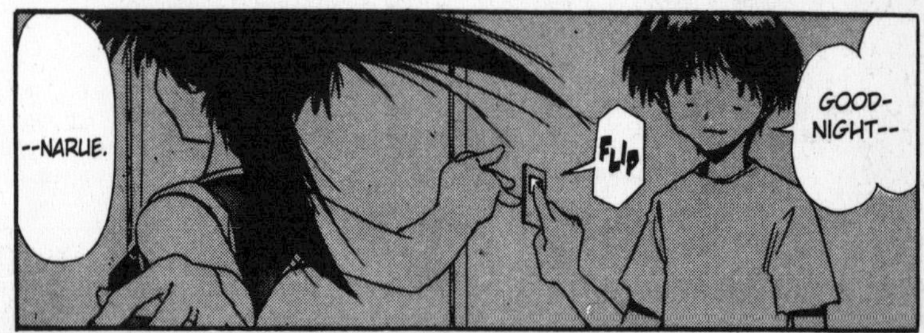
GOOD-NIGHT--
FLIP
--NARUE.

11 P.M.
くる TWIRL
くる TWIRL
くる TWIRL

2 A.M.

THANKS NARUE!
NOW I CAN'T SLEEP!

I'M SORRY.
HUH?

I MEANT TO STOP, BUT I WAS HAVING SO MUCH FUN--
--I GOT CARRIED AWAY.

I'M SORRY.
AH.
PAT

GOODNIGHT!
CRASH

End of Chapter

I'M KAZUTO IZUKA, AN ORDINARY MIDDLE SCHOOLER.
Mom 母
Sis ババア
Dad 父
Me ボク
BUT LIFE SEEMS ANYTHING BUT ORDINARY THESE DAYS.
MY GIRLFRIEND, NARUE NANASE, IS AN ALIEN.
KAZUTO, WAKE UP.
Squeeze
UH?
I'VE BECOME SO DESENSITIZED.
BREAK-FAST READY.
NOTHING REALLY SURPRISES ME ANYMORE.
EVEN IF I HAVE AN UN-FAMILIAR SISTER SPRING UP ONE MORNING.

Chapter 5: AN UNFAMILIAR SISTER

-- WHO SHE IS?

UM ...
SO WHO ARE ...
TWEET TWEET
AH.
GRAB
DOESN'T IT FEEL SO NICE WHEN YOU GET UP EARLY?
YOU BETTER THANK ME--
THUMP
-- SLEEPY-HEAD BROTHER!
WHY IS YOUR HEART BEATING? YOU DON'T KNOW WHO SHE IS, YOU IDIOT!
YOU'RE DATING NARUE!
THUMP THUMP
AH.
ばったり
RUN
NARUE!

Y... YOU'VE GOT IT ALL WRONG. SH... SH... SHE'S...
PLOP

MORNING.
Vreeem

FWOO

DING
DONG

KAZUTO.
I'VE BEEN LOOKING FOR YOU.
TAK TAK
TAK A

HEY... UH... WHAT'S YOUR NAME?
RIN ASAKURA.
I KNEW YOU WEREN'T MY SISTER.

RIN, ARE YOU ALSO AN ALIEN?
DO YOU HAVE ANY RELATIONS WITH NARUE?
WOW! HOW DID YOU KNOW?
WHAT ELSE AM I SUPPOSED TO THINK?
I'VE BEEN WATCHING YOU FROM THE STARSHIP.
I WANTED --
--TO EXPERIENCE WHAT LIFE ON EARTH WOULD BE LIKE. SO I CAME DOWN.
I HAVE NO ONE ELSE I CAN TURN TO! JUST FOR TODAY, PLEASE!
O... OKAY.
THANK YOU SO MUCH!

RIN!
I BROUGHT YOU SNACKS AND SOME JUICE!
TRIP
WHAT WAS *THAT* FOR, NARUE?
HEY.
MARUO, WHAT'S THAT?
HUH?
IT'S THE "LET'S SURROUND RIN ASAKURA, OUR IDOL" CLUB!
IDOL? THAT'S SO STUPID.

THAT GIRL... SHE'S ONLY LOOKING AT KAZUTO.
IT MUST BE MY IMAGINATION. WHO'D FALL FOR KAZUTO EXCEPT FOR ME?
I CLAIM THAT QUOTE.
SNAP
I'LL RELAY NARUE'S LOVE FOR KAZUTO --
WHAT?
WHAH HAH HAH HAH HAH
-- AND KICK HIM OUT OF THE RIN ASAKURA CLUB!
IF YOU DO THAT, YOU'RE DEAD.
URRRRR
...

THEY GAVE ME SO MANY SNACKS.
YOU'RE SO POPULAR, RIN.

DO YOU WANT ME ALL TO YOUR-SELF?

WHAT?!
パクッ
TOSS
GOTCHA!

YOU'RE BLUSHING. IT WAS A JOKE.
TAK
HUH?

DASH
HEY!
I WONDER IF THIS IS HOW IT'D BE IF I HAD A YOUNGER SISTER?
TRIP

LOOKS LIKE YOU'RE HAVING FUN.
SLAM
ARE YOU ALL RIGHT?
NARUE!
OH, LET ME INTRODUCE YOU. SHE'S A TRANS-FER STUDENT FROM OUTER SPACE.
I'M RIN ASAKURA. NICE TO MEET YOU.
NICE TO MEET YOU, TOO.
HUH?
I DIDN'T MEAN--
--TO DO THAT?
WHAT DO YOU WANT TO DO WITH KAZUTO?
I'M JUST SHOWING HER AROUND.
SHE'S AN ALIEN, TOO.
ARE YOU SAYING --

-- THAT I CAN'T HELP OTHER GIRLS EXCEPT FOR YOU?

YOU'RE RIGHT.

I'M SORRY I'M BEING SELFISH. HAVE FUN SHOWING HER AROUND.

YEAH ... I'LL SEE YOU TOMORROW.

ARE TREES RARE?
I CAN SEE THEM IN VIRTUAL REALITY, BUT THERE AREN'T ANY REAL TREES ON THE STAR-SHIP.

I'M GLAD. I WAS REALLY WORRIED IF I WAS GOING TO BE ABLE TO SHOW YOU AROUND EARTH.
THERE'S NO NEED TO WORRY.

YOU'RE SO KIND TO ME EVEN THOUGH YOU DON'T KNOW ME.
YOU DIDN'T EVEN FLINCH WHEN NARUE TOLD YOU SHE'S AN ALIEN.

I'M JEALOUS OF NARUE.

I'M NOT NICE. I'M JUST TIMID. I'M SO ORDINARY.
NARUE DATES ME BUT I'M ALWAYS WORRIED IF I'M GOOD ENOUGH FOR HER.

THIS IS WHAT I THINK.

PEOPLE WHO THINK LOW OF THEMSELVES STRIVE FOR MORE.
THEY'RE UNWILLING TO GIVE UP AND IN THE END--
--THAT'S WHAT SHAPES THIS WORLD.
YOU'RE MORE AMAZING THAN YOU THINK--
--KAZUTO.

*INTERSPACE TELECOMMUNICATIONS

BRINGING NARUE NANASE TO OUR HOME PLANET IS OUR GOAL.
KAZUTO IZUKA IS THE ONE WHO HOLDS THE KEY.
WE CAN'T DO IT BY FORCE. HER HEART AND BODY MUST BE INTACT.
YOU MUST FOLLOW THE THREE LAWS AND ACT ACCORDINGLY.
YES... BUT WHY DO I HAVE TO PRETEND TO BE HIS YOUNGER SISTER?
LOVE MUST HAVE IMPACT.
JUST GO.
YES!
I AM --
KAZUTO!
-- MERELY FOLLOWING ORDERS.

VREEM
WHAT'S WRONG, NARUE?
HUFF
HUFF
INITIATE OPERATION!
KISS ME, KAZUTO.
HUH?
KISS ME.
THUMP
THUMP
THUMP
WHAT ... ARE YOU...?
I'M... DATING... NARU...
SHAKE
SHAKE
SHAKE
THUMP
THUMP
HE'S TOUGH.
YOU LOVE NARUE THAT MUCH?

B
HUH?
IT STOPPED.
OH NO!
THE CIRCUIT...
REEE
RIN!
ARE YOU ALL ...
DROP
WHOA!
KAZUTO!
THUD

vreen
TELEPORTATION!
I'M TOO LATE!
GWE
ONE. PRESERVE THYSELF.

TWO. OBEY THY ORDERS.
Gra
Flip

THRASH
crash
THREE. PROTECT ALL LIFE FORMS.
THE THREE ROBOT LAWS.

HUH?
CREAK
WHAT THE HECK WAS THAT?

LEAVE.
GWE

YES ...
CAN YOU STAND?

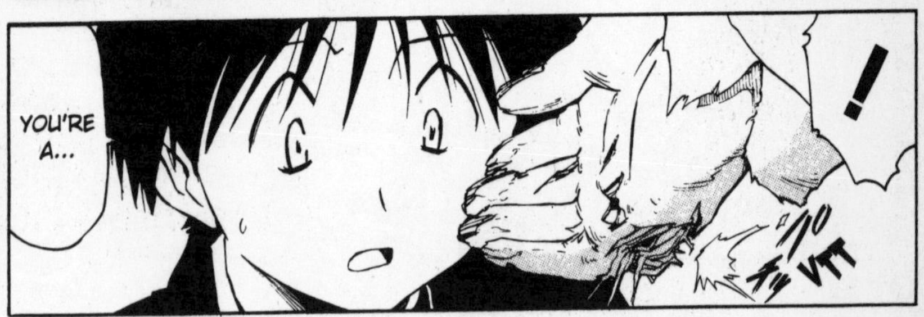
!
VTT
YOU'RE A...

I'M A MECH THAT WAS SENT BY THE INSPECTION BUREAU--
VTT
--TO SEPARATE YOU AND NARUE.

THE EMOTIONS YOU WERE FEELING TOWARDS ME ARE FALSE.
I FOLLOWED YOUR PSYCHOLOGICAL PROFILE --
--AND PLAYED YOUR PERFECT GIRL.
SO YOU TRICKED ME?
... YES.
BUT IT WASN'T ALL LIES.
I WAS ABLE TO CONTROL EVERYONE USING MY MIND CONTROL PULSE--
-- EXCEPT FOR YOU.
I DIDN'T LIE IN THE PARK.
YOU'RE MORE AMAZING THAN YOU THINK.

監察庁
inspection bureau
GWWW
I HOPE --
-- TO SEE YOU AGAIN, NOT BY ORDERS.
NARUE.
I WISH YOU HAP-PINESS WITH KAZUTO.
VREEM

I'M SORRY.
IT'S ALL MY FAULT.
IT'S OKAY.
IF A ROBOT THAT LOOKED EXACTLY LIKE YOU SHOWED UP I'D PROBABLY...
BUT I MADE YOU FEEL SO TER-RIBLE.
THEN CLOSE YOUR EYES.
Haaa
AND LOCK YOUR JAW.
DO IT!
clench

End of Chapter

I'M KAZUTO IZUKA, AN ORDINARY MIDDLE SCHOOLER.
BUT MY GIRLFRIEND, NARUE NANASE, IS AN ALIEN.
LATELY WE'VE GOTTEN A LOT CLOSER AND --
DAMN IT!
I OVER SLEPT!
--WE'VE DECIDED TO WALK TO SCHOOL TOGETHER EVERY MORNING.
TAK
TAK
SORRY I'M LATE.
HA HA
YOU'RE DEAD! HA HA, JUST KIDDING.
TK TK
BEING LATE AND TOLLS ARE NON-EXISTANT TO ME.

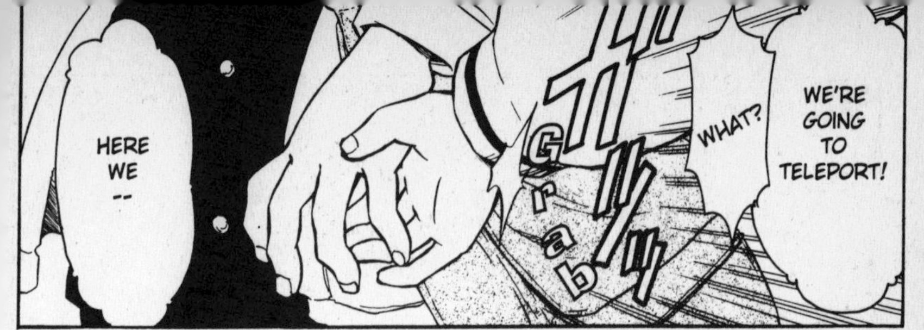

Chapter 6: THE LOST HEADBAND

--GO!

!?
AAAAA!
THUD
WHOA.
HEY! ARE YOU ALL RIGHT?
I THINK SO ...
NARUE!

MOVE OUTTA THE WAY!

DGDGDGDG

NARUE.

BLUSH

I WONDER WHAT'S WRONG?

TILT

SLIP

Tnk

IT'S A MINOR CUN-CUSSION.

FWT
DON'T WORRY ABOUT HER. YOU CAN GET BACK TO CLASS.

MY *HEAD-BAND!*
IT'S MISSING!

HEAD-BAND?
YOU KNOW, THE THING THAT PULLS HER HAIR BACK.
MAYBE IT FELL OFF ON THE WAY TO THE INFIRMARY.

CLASS IS GOING TO START. LET'S LOOK FOR IT LATER. IT MIGHT BE AT THE LOST AND FOUND.
OKAY.

YOU CAN DO IT!
COME ON!
SHAKE SHAKE
YOU'RE ONLY GIVING HER BACK HER HEADBAND!
CLINCH

--NARUE WAS DIFFERENT.
HERE.
AND I FELL IN LOVE WITH HER.

BUT I'M SURE --
--I'LL NEVER TELL HER HOW I FEEL.

UH... UMM ...
ドキ THUMP
ドキ THUMP
N... NARUE ?

WHAT IS IT?
NITTA.
SQUEEZE

N... N... N...
カァァァ
Blush
?

NOTHING!
ダッ
DASH

I CAN'T BELIEVE MYSELF!
I'M SUCH A COWARD!

しかも体育

During Gym Class

YOU'RE A GUY, BUT YOU SURE KNOW A LOT.

I HAVE A YOUNGER SISTER SO...

Hah-ha

PASS

WHY DO YOU CARRY ONE AROUND?

HAH HAH HAH!
WHY'D I ASK ...
VWOOOM
CIAO!

NOT HERE ...

NOT HERE ...
Lost and Found

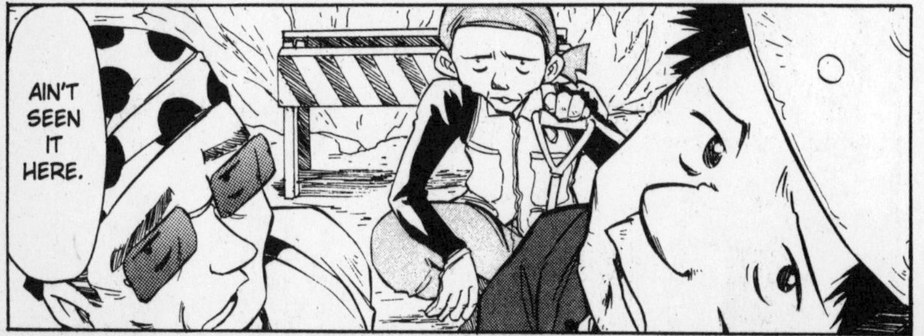
AIN'T SEEN IT HERE.

SIGH ... WHERE COULD IT BE?
UM... HOW ABOUT THIS INSTEAD?
RUSTLE RUSTLE

A RIBBON? THAT WON'T DO.

THAT HEADBAND IS REALLY A CONNECTOR.
IT LINKS ME WITH THE STARSHIPS IN ORBIT AND LETS ME TELEPORT.

SO IT'S A HIGH-TECH ITEM... DO YOU HAVE A SPARE AT HOME?
I DO, BUT ...

THEN IT'S FINE. WEAR THIS UNTIL YOU GET HOME.

WHAT IF SOMEONE EVIL GETS THEIR HANDS ON THE CONNECTOR?
THIS IS SERIOUS!

I DON'T WANT THAT RIBBON!
TAK
YOU CAN WEAR IT!
WHAT DO YOU WANT ME TO DO?
CLENCH

I'VE DECIDED.
I'M GOING TO PUT THIS IN HER LOCKER.
THAT'S THE BEST THING TO DO.

NARUE WEARS THIS EVERY-DAY.
Thump
Thump
...
...
Fst
THIS FEELS WEIRD.
HEH HEH

BUT IF SHE FINDS OUT I PUT IT ON?
WHY ARE YOU WEARING A GIRL'S HEADBAND?
PERVERT.
DIE FREAK.

NO! NO!
squeeze
I DON'T WANT THAT!

I CAN'T --
-- GET IT OFF.

HEY, KAZUTO.
Rummage
Rummage
I DOUBT SHE REALLY MEANT FOR YOU TO WEAR IT.

I CAN'T TELL IF YOU'RE LOYAL OR AN IDIOT.
LOOK! THAT'S SO CUTE!
CHUCKLE CHUCKLE
I WANT TO WEAR IT SO LEAVE ME ALONE!

I'M NOT GOING TO HELP AN IDIOT WHO'D GO THIS FAR FOR A WOMAN.
I'M NOT GOING TO HELP YOU, BUT YOU NEED TO GET RECOGNITION.
RIGHT, NARUE?
666

KAZUTO ...
I CAN'T FIND IT.
I'VE LOOKED EVERY-WHERE BUT...
SHWINK
シュルッ
UM... HOW DOES IT LOOK?
?
TOO CUTE!
BVV

GOD! BUDDAH! WHOEVER!
PEEK
PLEASE DON'T LET ME BUMP INTO NARUE.
PEEK
AH.
BUMP
HI NITTA.
WHAT ARE YOU WEARING?
SHE'S GONNA KNOW.
SHORTY.
PERVERT.
UHH ...
UH ...
SHE'S GONNA KNOW.
YOU'RE A GUY.
SHE'S GONNA KNOW!
AAAH!
VREEM
TELEPORTATION?
WOOO

I'M SO JEALOUS, MR. KANEHARA.
ISN'T IT A BEAUTY?
I BOUGHT THE NEWEST SHINIEST MODEL ...
MY CAR!
AHH!
THIS WAY!
VREEM
TAK TAK
VREEM
STOMP
STOMP
WE'RE TOO LATE!
MR. KANEHARA! MR. KANEHARA!
THE CONNECTOR SYNCHRONIZES WITH ITS WEARER AND FOLLOWS THEIR WISH.

Dshhh
HE NEEDS TO CALM DOWN.
AAAAA!
EEEEK!
VREEM
AHHH!
VREEM

AAAAAA!

STAY CALM! WE'LL SAVE YOU!

NO!

I DON'T WANT NARUE TO SEE ME LIKE THIS!

I'D RATHER FALL!

!?

KAZUTO, LISTEN.

Mumble Mumble

HUH?

STALL?

I'M COMING SO DON'T LET GO!
WHY'D YOU PUT ON THE HEADBAND IF YOU'RE A GUY?
I SHOULDN'T TALK THOUGH.
KLANK
I WANTED TO GET CLOSE TO NARUE.
I WANTED TO HELP BY GIVING HER BACK WHAT SHE LOST.
BECAUSE I LOVE NARUE!
BUT I COULDN'T DO IT.
COWARDS LIKE ME--
--SHOULDN'T *BE* IN LOVE!
DO YOU REALLY BELIEVE THAT?

IT'S BETTER TO BE HELPFUL TO THE PEOPLE YOU LOVE THAN NOT TO BE.

EVEN IF YOU CAN'T DO ANYTHING YOU SHOULDN'T DENY HOW YOU FEEL.

BUT JUST SO YOU KNOW, I'M NARUE'S BOYFRIEND.
KAZUTO ...
COME ON. CLIMB BACK UP.
I CAN'T ...
I JUST REMEMBERED.
HUH?
I CAN'T EVEN DO ONE PULL-UP.
SLIDE
HEY! HEY! HEY!
AR!
AAAAH!
CLINK

Jump
Grab
FWOON
TKK TKK TKK TKK
PSS
VREE
FWK

NARUE!
VREEM
DROP
GAH!
...
ARE YOU ALL RIGHT, NITTA?
THANKS FOR FINDING IT. I'M SORRY YOU HAD TO GO THROUGH THAT.
I...
smile
I'M FINE.
SO... UM...

End of Chapter

I'M KAZUTA IZUKA, AN ORDINARY MIDDLE SCHOOLER.
MY GIRLFRIEND NARUE NANASE IS AN **ALIEN.**
WHY ARE YOU SO HAPPY?
MY SISTER'S SOON COMING TO EARTH TO VISIT ME AND MY DAD!
IT'S BEEN THE TWO OF US SINCE MY MOM DIED, SO I'M REALLY HAPPY!
I DIDN'T KNOW YOUR MOTHER --
OH, STOP IT!
Slap Slap
STOP MAKING THAT SAD FACE.
COUGH COUGH

Chapter 7: MY SISTER'S HERE! (PART I)

SHE PUSHED ME HARD.
I WONDER WHAT KIND OF PEOPLE HER PARENTS ARE!

SO, WHAT DOES YOUR SISTER LOOK LIKE?
I'VE NEVER MET HER SO I DON'T KNOW.

SHE'S TWENTY-SIX AND SHE'S A HUNDRED PERCENT GALACTIAN.
OH, YOU'RE NARUE'S FRIEND?
TWENTY-SIX ...
JUST SO YOU KNOW, MY MOTHER WAS MY DAD'S SECOND WIFE AND...
Currently in La-La Land
HEY!
HUH?
WEL-COME BACK.

A... ANYWAY ...
Hah Hah Hah
あはは
I'M SURE SHE'S A NICE PERSON.

YEAH.

ガチャ
CREAK
I'M HOME.
WHAT THE ...
DAD NEEDS TO STOP LEAVING HIS CLOTHES EVERYWHERE.
ざっしざっし
GSH GSH
ガチャ
CREAK
SHH
ゴウンゴウン
VYM VYM
GOOD EVENING, NARUE.
カラカラ
SLIDE
GOOD EVENING MR. LANDLORD.
ゴウンゴウン
VYM VYM

WHEN I SEE YOU WORKING HARD--
感心 感心
GOOD GIRL
--YOU REMIND ME OF MY LATE WIFE.
ふ～う
PHEW
I WONDER IF SIS IS GOOD AT HOUSE-WORK?
UH...
THANK YOU!
KEEP UP THE GOOD WORK.
SLIDE
IT'D BE SO MUCH FUN TO GO SHOP-PING--
NARUE'S IMAGINA-TION.
--AND COOK TOGETHER.
RUSTLE
VYM VYM VYM
I HOPE SHE'S NICE!
PAPA, I'M COMING HOME KANAKA
I'M HOME!
EW!
SPLASH

DAD!
だらぁ〜
SOAKED
WHAT HAPPENED TO YOU?
THE PAINT BUCKET TIPPED AT THE CONSTRUCTION SITE. ON THE WAY HOME I GOT CHASED BY A DOG AND FELL IN THE SEWAGE DRAIN.
I THOUGHT THAT ONLY HAPPENED IN OLD MANGA GRAPHIC NOVELS.
HURRY AND GET CHANGED. YOU CAN'T MEET HER LIKE THIS.
MEET WHO?
JEEZ, SIS! WHO ELSE?
ギクッ
UH OH
NO ... FORGET IT.
YOU'RE SO STRANGE, DAD.
トボトボ
TOK TOK
I WANT TO TALK TO YOU ABOUT THAT...
HUH?

GO GET SOME MACKEREL! MACKEREL, OKAY?
OKAY, OKAY.
IT'S ON SALE AT BONZAI SUPER-MARKET!
JEEZ.
BEEP BEEP
I HEARD YOU THE FIRST TIME.
!!
VWOOOO
THAT'S THE RUDE GIRL FROM THIS MORNING.
WHY IS SHE ALL THE WAY UP THERE?

SHE TELE- PORTED?!
REE
BONK
ATTENTION: NEVER USE TELE- PORTATION FOR EVIL PURPOSES.
YOU'RE KILLING ME!
SKID
I SWEAR YOU ALMOST KILLED ME!
OWW

MISTER, YOU'RE FOLLOW-ING ME.

IT WAS A COINCIDENCE! IF YOU SAW A GIRL ON TOP OF A TELEPHONE POLE YOU'D BE WORRIED TOO!

HUG

AH!

WHAT'S THIS FOR?

TELEPORTATION AND THIS WEIRD CONVERSATION ... IT'S LIKE--
LET'S SEE ...
--IS THIS TWERP NARUE'S SISTER?

HEY, MISTER!
DON'T CALL ME MISTER!

I'M LOOKING FOR MY DAD. HE'S THE DIPLOMAT FROM PLANET JAPAN. HE'S A SUPER ELITE AND MAKES OVER FIFTEEN MILLION YEN FOR HIS SALARY.
HIS NAME IS TADASHI NANASE.

NANASE?!
DO YOU KNOW HIM? TAKE ME!

I HEARD HE LIVES AROUND HERE, BUT--
--I HEARD THERE ARE ONLY RUNDOWN APARTMENTS IN THIS AREA.
...

HERE WE ARE.

YOU'RE LYING!
SHOCK
NOPE. HE LIVES ON THE SECOND FLOOR.

I GET IT.
IT'S TEMPORARY HOUSING UNTIL WE MOVE INTO A MANSION TOGETHER!
HELLO?
I WOULDN'T GET YOUR HOPES UP...

WHAT?
NO, NOTHING.

I NEED TO GO BECAUSE I WAS ON MY WAY TO GET SOME MACKEREL.
THANKS MISTER!

THERE'S NO *WAY* SHE'S NARUE'S OLDER SISTER.
I'LL ASK NARUE LATER.

KNOCK
YES?
THUMP THUMP
CREAK
PAPA!
IT'S BEEN SO LONG!
HUG
WHO ARE YOU?
KANAKA!
PAPA!?

KANAKA?
"PAPA" ...?!

YOU RE-MARRIED?
YES.

I'M **NOT** GOING --
GLARE

--TO CONSIDER SUCH--
--A YOUNG WOMAN AS MY **MOTHER!**
ZOW

HUH?
KANAKA!
VREE

...
GRATA
GRATA
FWOOO
YOU'VE GOT IT ALL WRONG!
COME BACK!

I HAVE A QUESTION.

TWEEE

WHAT KIND OF MORAL CODE DOES THIS PLANET FOLLOW?

HOW SHOULD *I* KNOW!

DASH

VREE
WAIT, MISTER!
PSYCHE!
TURN
SLAM
SHE CAN'T TELEPORT AS WELL AS NARUE.
I CAN OUT-RUN HER.
DRIBBLE
YOU'RE NOT GET-TING AWAY!
BATHY-SCAPHE!
PJSS287
VWOOM
*BATHYSCAPHE

VWOOSH
TOONK
TOONK
TOONK
BATHYSCAPHE! EXECUTE TRANSFER!
VREE
AS YOU WISH.

THUD
OUCH!
I'M TRAPPED INSIDE A SPACESHIP?
GGG
GGG
GOOD JOB, BATHYSCAPHE!
TORTURE HIM SO HE TELLS US WHAT HE KNOWS ABOUT PAPA!
NO WAY!
YOU MEAN INTERROGATE.
OH, RIGHT.
THERE'S NO NEED TO INTERROGATE HIM.
WE'LL ASK THE NEARBY STARSHIPS.
CALL
Confidential
VWW
VWW

LONG TIME NO SEE, BATHY-SCAPHE.
IT'S BEEN AWHILE, HAKATAZE HOLNICH.
UM ...
I NEED YOUR REPLIES IMMEDIATELY.

THE BOY YOU TRANSFERRED IS LADY KANAKA'S YOUNGER SISTER NARUE'S CLASSMATE AND BOYFRIEND.
MY YOUNGER SISTER!?

YOUR FATHER REMARRIED A WOMAN FROM EARTH AND LADY NARUE--
--WAS BORN BETWEEN THEM.

NARUE'S MOM WAS AN EARTH PERSON!
THEN THE WOMAN AT THE APARTMENT WAS NARUE?

THAT'S NOT THE POINT! WHY IS MY YOUNGER SISTER OLDER THAN ME!?

THAT'S BECAUSE --

--OF THE TIME LAG EFFECT.

FIFTEEN YEARS AGO --

-- I PASSED THROUGH THE STARGATES THAT CONNECT THE STARS, JUST TO COME TO EARTH.

ZWOOO

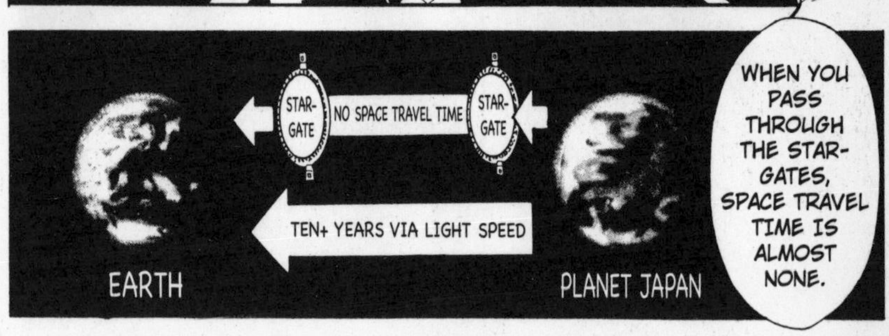

KANAKA RAN AWAY FROM HOME WHEN SHE WAS TWELVE, FOLLOWING ME.

SHE SMUGGLED ON A CARGO-SHIP THAT DOESN'T PASS THROUGH THE STARGATES.

SHE WAS LATER SAVED BY BATHY-SCAPHE, BUT THE PROBLEM REMAINED.

TIME MOVES SLOWER INSIDE A STARSHIP THAT TRAVELS FASTER THAN LIGHT.
THAT'S THE TIME LAG EFFECT.

WHILE KANAKA WAS TRAVELING, FIFTEEN YEARS HAD PASSED ON EARTH.

THATS WHY ON THE OUTSIDE YOU LOOK LIKE THE OLDER SISTER.

RING RING
STARTLE

HELLO?
IT'S KANAKA.

I HAVE YOUR BOY-FRIEND IN CAPTIVITY.
KAZUTO'S THERE?
I'M HUNGRY

SIS?
DON'T CALL ME SIS!

I'LL TRADE YOUR BOY-FRIEND --
-- FOR PAPA.

OKAY!
QUICK DECISION
NARUE . . .
CRY

IF YOU WERE ON TOP OF THIS, THIS WOULDN'T HAVE HAPPENED!
SORRY.

VROOOOO
FWOO
ZWOO
BATHY-SCAPHE!
REASSEMBLE THE STARSHIP TO MATCH THE AREA HOUSING.
AS YOU WISH.
YWOOOO
CRK
CRK
CRK
POOF

BOOM
THE STARSHIP TURNED INTO A HOUSE.
KANAKA!

IN THE MIDST OF CONFUSION...
WHAT AM I GOING TO DO ABOUT THE MACK-EREL?
TO BE CON-TINUED.

CHAPTER 8: MY SISTER'S HERE!

CHAPTER 8: MY SISTER'S HERE! (PART 2)

OH, THAT'S RIGHT! PAPA, SUSHI'S YOUR FAVORITE RIGHT?
HELLO? CAN WE GET TWO DELUXE SUSHI PLATTERS DELIVERED?
SHOCK
DELUXE?
BATHY-SCAPHE'S SAFE AND COMPLETELY FULL!
KISS BEING POOR GOODBYE AND--
BEEP
ST&T
--AND WE'LL LIVE TOGETH-HUH?
YOU DON'T NEED TO DO ANYTHING.
I'M JUST HAPPY YOU WERE SAFE.

NARUE ...
I'M FINE.

THE SUPERMARKET CLOSES AT NINE. I WONDER WHAT TIME IT IS?
CRK
IT'S SEVEN THIRTY EXACTLY.
AAAAHH!
CRK
CRK

I'M SORRY I SCARED YOU. I AM BATHY-SCAPHE, A DEEP DIMENSIONAL CONVOY.
CONVOY? A SHIP?
YOU LOOK HUMAN TO ME.
DO WHATEVER WITH ME.
NO, I'M A STAR-SHIP.

I'M SURE YOU KNOW THE SITUATION THROUGH THE INTERNAL SPEAKERS.
THE SITUATION IS COMPLICATED, BUT THEY'RE FAMILY.
PAT PAT
IT'S BETTER TO GET ALONG THAN TO FIGHT.

YOU MIGHT BE--
-- ABLE TO UNTIE THE TANGLED THREADS OF FATE.
HUH?

BATHY-SCAPHE! GET RID OF THE OLD MAN!
SHE PISSES ME OFF.
I'M SORRY.

ギュルッ
GWEE
THE SHIP'S EXIT IS OVER HERE.
カラカラ
KLAK KLAK
HOW IS THIS A SHIP?
KAZUTO, I'M SO SORRY!
SOUNDS LIKE YOU HAVE A HANDFUL WITH YOUR SISTER.
I'M REALLY SORRY!
I HAVE TO GO TO THE SUPER-MARKET --
-- SO I NEED TO GO--
キュッ
TUG
-- BUT --
...

ARRRR!! I'M HUNGRY!
WHERE DID HE RUN OFF TO?
I'M GOING TO KILL KAZUTO!
TNK
TNK
TNK

I'M HOME. I BROUGHT SUSHI.
GOOD JOB, DAD!

WHAT? YOU GUYS ARE EATING SUSHI?
WE SAVED YOU SOME.
I DON'T CARE ABOUT THAT.
I'M JUST CALLING TO TELL YOU I'M AT MY FRIEND'S HOUSE.

だははは
HA HA HA
ヒック
HIC
KAZUTO... I BET YOU'RE DOING SOMETHING NAUGHTY WITH A GIRL.
WHAT?!
ATOMIC DRY

HA HA!!
GOTCHA! JUST KIDDING!
KLAK
SIGH ...

HERE'S SOME TEA.
OH, THANKS.

...

IT'S PRETTY POINTLESS FOR ME TO BE HERE.
SIP
IT'S STRANGE WITH JUST US TWO.

JUST US TWO!!
KAZUTO.
LET'S DO SOME-THING NAUGHTY ...
SPAT

PAT PAT
DASH

IT'S SNOW-ING.
HEY! I'M GOOD TO GO!

WHAT'S WRONG?
I'M JUST GETTING SOME FRESH AIR!
DRIBBLE
DRIBBLE

TICK TOCK TICK TOCK
BONG
BONG
THAT'S NOT A WATER PIPE! THAT'S A HOLLOW FISH PATTY!
LAUGH

BONG
BONG
PEEK

MAC-ARONI?
IT'S MELT-ING! IT'S MELT-ING!

WHAT KIND OF A PERSON WAS YOUR MOTHER?
HUH?

SHE WAS AN ORDINARY WOMAN.
SHE WOULD FALL IN LOVE WITH FLOWERS, POEMS, CLOUDS, ANYTHING!
SHE USED TO HUG ME ALL THE TIME.
THAT MEANS SHE REALLY LOVED YOU.
I'M SURE SHE COULDN'T EXPRESS EVERYTHING HOW SHE FELT WITH WORDS.
...
I'VE DECIDED.
EH?

HUG
I'M GOING TO--
--SEE MY SISTER.
NARUE.

WERE YOU SAD YOU DIDN'T GET TO SEE ME?
YEAH.
FIFTEEN YEARS WAS A LONG TIME--
--BUT I HAD NARUE SO ...
HMF

FORGET ABOUT THAT!
I WANT TO SIT ON YOUR LAP!
HUG

YOU GETTING TOO OLD FOR THIS.
YOUR HEAVy...
重い…
I'M NOT OLD. I'M STILL A KID.

PLUS NO ONE'S LOOKING ...

!!

WHAT'S WRONG?
YOU'RE NOT MY PAPA.
THOSE AREN'T--
--MY PAPA'S HANDS!
DAS
KANAKA!
STUB

FATHER, NEVER THERE WHEN WE NEED YOU MOST.
BY: NARUE
OWWW!
バタバタ
PAT PAT
!
SLAM
SIS!
WAIT!
VREE
NARUE!
VREE

VWOO
VREE
SPAT
!!
VNNN
VREEEM

THAT'S NOT TRUE.

YOU HAVE US.

STOP ACTING NICE!

YOU'RE GONNA LEAVE ME IN THE END ANYWAY!

YOU SHOULDN'T HAVE THIS!

GRAB

DON'T TOUCH ME!

STOP!

VZZZ

STOP IT!

VSH

THE SELF-DEFENSE GUN WILL ROB THE OPPONENT'S ENERGY IMMEDIATELY.
ANYONE WHO GETS SHOT WILL EXPERIENCE A CONDITION SIMILAR TO A FEVER.
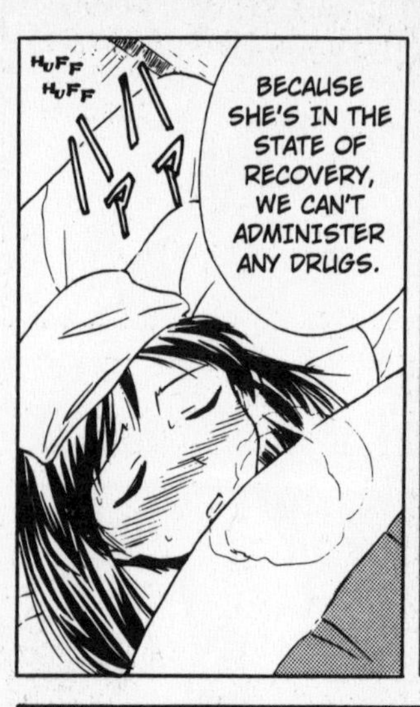
BECAUSE SHE'S IN THE STATE OF RECOVERY, WE CAN'T ADMINISTER ANY DRUGS.
HUFF HUFF
HA HA

WHY DID YOU SHOOT HER? SHE WAS LOOKING FORWARD TO SEEING YOU.
YOU LIE.

THE ONLY ONE WHO CAME TO SAVE ME WHEN I WAS ON THE CARGO SHIP WAS BATHY-SCAPHE.
EVEN TV SAID--
--PEOPLE ONLY CARE ABOUT THEM-SELVES.

THAT'S NON-SENSE!
SLAM

THAT'S BE-CAUSE --

--HE'S SERIOUSLY WORRIED ABOUT YOU.

I HAVE A MESSAGE FOR YOU.

GLOW

AS YOU DID KANAKA --

-- I ALSO SUFFER FROM THE TIME LAG EFFECT EVERY TIME I TRAVEL.

EVERY TIME I COME HOME AFTER A TRIP, YOU'RE OLDER AND SEEM SO DISTANT.

I HAVE NO ONE ELSE TO BLAME BUT MYSELF BECAUSE I CAN'T GIVE UP MY WORK.

MISTER.
HUH?

WAS NARUE WAITING FOR ME?
YEAH.

REALLY?
YES.

KANAKA ...

FWOOO

SNORE
ZZZZ

チュン
TWEET
チュン
TWEET

チュン
TWEET TWEET
チュン
...
SIS ...?
AH ...
YOU WERE AWAKE THE WHOLE TIME?
IT WAS MY FAULT SO ...
I'M SORRY, NARUE.
YOU'RE IT, SIS.

THUS, NARUE NOW HAS AN OLDER YOUNGER SISTER.

YOU CAN DO IT WITH HIM.

HUH?

THE MORNING FELT SO BLISSFUL --

ZZZ

--I LAZILY SLEPT UNTIL NOON THAT DAY.

End of Chapter

I'M KAZUTO IZUKA, A NORMAL MIDDLE SCHOOLER.
MY GIRLFRIEND, NARUE NANASE, IS AN ALIEN.
ARE YOU DOWN TODAY, KAZUTO?
YEAH... NARUE DIDN'T COME TO SCHOOL TODAY.
TRICKLE
TRICKLE
MAYBE SHE'S SICK.
KAZUTO.
EEK
EEK
DID YOU HEAR THAT?
Y... YEAH.
IT WAS FROM THE STALL.

Chapter 9: NARUE SOS

YES! I'M SAVED.

BAM

SLAM
I ALWAYS THOUGHT --
-- NARUE WAS A WEIRDO, BUT SHE'S ACTUALLY --
--A *MUSHROOM* ALIEN!
I DON'T SPROUT!
I TELEPORTED AND I GOT STUCK IN THE RIFTS BETWEEN THE SUPER DIMENSIONS.
I CAN'T GET OUT.
I DON'T KNOW WHAT A SUPER DIMENSION IS, BUT --
-- WHAT'S ON THE OTHER SIDE OF THAT WALL?
THE GIRL'S BATHROOM *STALL!*

PEOPLE WILL *PANIC* IF THEY SEE THIS!

I HAVE A GREAT IDEA TO STALL SOME TIME.

SOMEONE WILL INFILTRATE THE GIRL'S BATHROOM.

LOCK THE STALL FROM THE INSIDE AND CREEP OVER THE WALL AND ESCAPE.

Girl's bathroom

MAKE SURE YOU LOCK THIS STALL FROM THE *INSIDE.*

ROGER!

NOOOOO!

CLINCH

Uffff
A FAVOR?
I'M SICK SO I CAN'T DO MUCH.
ゴホ ゴホ
Cough Cough
IT'S NOT THAT BIG.
WE WANT TO--
CRACK
--BORROW YOUR UNIFORM.
I'M NOT DOING IT EVEN IF I'M IN DISGUISE.
Ding Dong
SECOND PERIOD'S STARTING.
Hajime's Punch & slap
八木に殴られた
AH!
DAMN.
Girl's bathroom
Chatter Chatter

Girl's bathro
THEY'RE ALL SKIPPING CLASS?
OH NO! SOMEONE'S HEADED TOWARDS A STALL!
ワイワイ
chitter chitter
WHICH ONE IS NARUE IN?
THE LAST ONE.

DON'T GO IN THE LAST ONE! DON'T GO IN THE LAST ONE! ***DON'T GO IN THE LAST ONE!***

CREAK
YES!!

ジ〜ロ〜
STARE

WHOOPS! I THOUGHT THAT WAS THE **BOYS** BATHROOM!
KARATE CHOP
YOU'RE SO SILLY! THE GIRLS WOULD HAVE ***KILLED*** US IF WE WENT IN!

...
TOKO
TOKO

NOW'S OUR CHANCE!
RUN
GOT IT!

SLAM

SLAM

HE'S ROLE-PLAYING BECAUSE HE'S EMBAR-RASSED ...
ZOW
ZOW
I THOUGHT HE LOST IT FOR A MOMENT ...

BVVV
SHUT
CLICK
Fsm
...
ガタ
IMB
WHERE'S YOUR SHIRT?
DON'T ASK.

CAN YOUR SISTER TELEPORT TOO?

YEAH.

WE SHOULD HAVE CALLED HER IN THE FIRST PLACE.

Girl's bathroom sneaker

STAB!

Idiot

CREAK!

THANKS FOR YOUR SHIRT.
!!!
OH, SURE.
I'M SORRY.
I KEEP DRAGGING YOU INTO MY MESS.
DON'T WORRY ABOUT IT.
RIGHT NOW I FEEL LIKE WE'RE UP TO NO GOOD. IT'S *FUN*.
CHICKLE
NARUE ...
PLOP
WHAT DO YOU THINK YOU'RE DOING IN HERE!?
VREEM
Asakura

RIN!
LONG TIME NO SEE!
I RECEIVED A RED ALERT FROM THE TRANSFER MANAGEMENT CONVOY SO I CAME TO HELP!
WAIT A MINUTE!
SHWINK
Inspection bureau
THIS POCKET IS CONNECTED TO THE FOURTH DIMENSION.
NOT THAT.
THE SCHOOL UNIFORM IS MEANT TO BE A DISGUISE.
Inspection bureau
NOT THAT EITHER.
WHAT ARE YOU GOING --
Gleam
-- TO DO WITH THAT SAW?

THIS IS A SUPER DIMENSIONAL SEPARATOR.
YOU'RE STUCK BETWEEN DIMENSIONS SO--

--I'M GOING TO CUT YOU IN TWO AND GET YOU OUT!
NO!

WHY ARE YOU AFRAID? YOUR BODY ALWAYS DISINTEGRATES WHEN YOU TELEPORT.
IT'S INSTINCTUAL!

THERE IS NO PAIN!
COMPLETELY SAFE
絶対安全
INSTANT DEATH?

NARUE, ARE YOU ALL RIGHT?
KNOCK
KNOCK
IT'S KANAKA.

YOUR BIG SISTER GOING TO HELP YOU? ARE YOU SURE?
YES! YES!
SHUT UP, MONKEY-FACE!

WHAT'S WRONG?
CREAK

PFF
SIS!

SHE CAN'T STOP LAUGHING.
SHE'S NO HELP.
SHAKE SHAKE
B... BATHROOM... GROWING OUT OF WALL...
HEH HEH...

I DEFINITELY HAVE A FEVER...
cough
LET'S CUT HER.
creak
WHAT ARE THEY DOING IN THERE?
MARUO, STOP HER!
Slam!
NOOO!
...
WHAT THE HECK?
STRUGGLE
STRUGGLE

Kween
I CAN'T BELIEVE HOW STRONG SHE IS.
I'M A MECH!
MONKEY FACE...!
HEH HEH HEH
EEK!
WOOOP
NARUE!
BFFF
NARUE... GOOD TIMING.
Hff
Hff
sway
sway
TELL OUR TEACHER I WENT HOME EARLY.

NARUE'S BUTT WAS STUCK --
ALL WE HAD TO DO WAS *PULL*?
-- IN THE RIFTS BETWEEN THE DIMENSIONS?

HER BUTT ...HEH HEH...
...

GUYS...

SHOCK
THE BATHROOM ISN'T A PLAYGROUND, YOU KNOW.
TWITCH TWITCH
Inspection bureau

THERE OUGHT TO BE A LIMIT TO HOW MUCH WEIRDNESS ONE SHOULD TAKE IN A DAY.
MY AFTERTHOUGHT WAS, I SHOULD TRY TO SPEND MY SCHOOLDAYS MORE GRACEFULLY.

THIS MANGA IS BROUGHT TO YOU UNPLANNED AND FRESHLY CONJURED UP EVERY MONTH BY THE MANGA ARTIST. PLEASE FORGIVE ME IF THERE ARE TERMS AND SETTING INCONSISTENCIES.

The Victims of This Volume

THE FINAL TOUCH HELPERS

YOUNGER SISTERS (BIOLOGICALLY RELATED)

YOUNGER BROTHER (BIOLOGICALLY RELATED)

Cover Wrap Illustration

MAKOTO ODAGI (AND ALL HE GOT WAS FOOD)

Continued in Volume 2

Bonus Theater:
You can do it, Boy!
SHE'S LATE.
IF SHE DOESN'T GET HERE SOON, WE'RE GOING TO BE LATE.
VREEM
I'M SORRY, KAZUTO!
IT'S OKAY.
WE'LL MAKE IT IF WE RUN.
IF WE TELEPORT ...
NO! WHAT IF YOU GET STUCK IN THE BATHROOM AGAIN?
YOU'RE RIGHT.
LET'S HURRY THEN!
YEAH ...
TAK
!!

HER SKIRT IS STUCK IN THE WAIST AREA!

?

ARE YOU COMMING?

POSE

I'M RIGHT BEHIND YOU!

HOW ARE YOU NOT REALIZING IT? YOUR SKIRT'S PRETTY SHORT.

MAYBE SHE WAS HALF ASLEEP WHEN SHE WAS CHANGING?

ARH.

ANYWAY!!

I CAN'T LET HER GO TO SCHOOL LIKE THAT!

PLAN A: BE A GENTLEMAN AND TELL HER UP FRONT.

MY LADY, YOUR SKIRT IS...

OH...

THIS IS TOO AWKWARD.

PLAN B: FIX HER SKIRT SWIFTLY, LIKE THE WIND.

Flip

DASH

PLAN B IT IS!!

RAHHHH!
INTERNAL SCREAMS
HEY! IT'S A CATFISH!!
MEOW
HALT
SLAP
Eeeee
KAZUTO!
FIST
I'M SORRY! I'M SORRY! I'M SORRY!

ZUNK
YOU'RE MY BOYFRIEND BUT--
--NOT UNTIL WE'RE ADULTS!
NO
?
SWOON
SHE...
SHE'S TOO CUTE!
Bang
Bang
KAZUTO! ARE YOU OKAY?
Bang
DROP
AND THEY WERE LATE TO SCHOOL.
CHECK US OUT IN BOOK 2...
STILL SHOWING

Q&A with Tomohiro Marukawa

CPM: In an average day, how do you spend your time? For example, what time do you start working?

Marukawa: I make the most progress when I work at night.

CPM: What was the most mysterious, intense experience you've had?

Marukawa: When I was an elementary student, I saw an orange UFO. It probably was an army aircraft that I had mistaken.

CPM: What kind of opportunity led you to your present career?

Marukawa: When I think back, I didn't spend much time being a manga fan. I just thought that I could achieve anything I wanted to.

CPM: Have you been writing manga since you were a student?

Marukawa: It wasn't until I became a "company man" that I began to write manga.

CPM: What kind of new pieces are you currently working on? What can we expect for your next project?

Marukawa: Currently, I'm drawing and working hard to finish *The World of Narue* series.

CPM: How did *The World of Narue* come to life? What was the production process?

Marukawa: I like Sci-Fi novels. Junior high school students don't read newspapers and books much and have an interest in Sci-Fi novels. With this in mind, I make these kinds of manga.

CPM: When you were creating *The World of Narue*, where did you get your inspiration?

Marukawa: I received my inspiration from the great American Sci-Fi Novels.

CPM: Other than the production of *The World of Narue*, what else do you think was very challenging?

Marukawa: Bringing this type of special theme and mixing it with daily Japanese life was very challenging. I wanted to use a method that makes people intrigued with the happy story. Dark and difficult stories alone are not interesting.

Q&A continued in

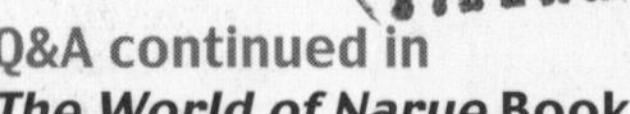

The World of Narue Book Two